CLASSICAL MELODIES FOR CHILDREN TO SING

A COLLECTION OF SONGS TAKEN FROM THE MUSIC OF GREAT COMPOSERS

BY MARY MARGARET CLARK

PAULIST PRESS
New York, N.Y./Paramus, N.J.

Design and Illustration: Gloria Ortiz
Music Transcription: Barbara Ledig
Art Direction: Jean Marie Hiesberger

Library of Congress
Catalogue Card Number: 75-42051

ISBN: 0-8091-1930-7

Published by
Paulist Press

Editorial Office:
1865 Broadway, New York, N.Y. 10023

Business Office:
400 Sette Drive, Paramus, N.J. 07652

Printed and bound in the
United States of America

CONTENTS

FOR SUMMER

OTHER SONGS FROM MUSIC OF GREAT COMPOSERS

The main purpose of this book is to promote an appreciation of the classics. If the teacher finds some of the melodies difficult to sing, it should be remembered that while perfection in performance is always a desirable goal, the prime purpose in any given melody in this book is to help the child recognize the music and be able to identify the great composer from which it comes.

FOREWORD

One of the best ways to acquaint children with good music is to have them sing melodies taken from the music of great composers. Once children have learned these melodies and can sing them, they will easily recognize and learn to appreciate these great compositions.

The use of this book has been a rewarding experience for me as a teacher. A week or so after the children in a class have learned a given song, it is a joy to watch their faces when they hear a symphonic recording of the melody they have been singing. They listen in a way they have not done before. Children can easily appreciate the classics if they are familiar with the main theme.

The piano accompaniments (with the exception of one or two) are written in simple form, easy enough for the classroom teacher to play, or for the junior pianist. Parents who also wish to instill in their children a love for music may find the book to be a valuable tool at home for fun and for learning.

Each song contains short facts concerning the life of the composer.

While the book may be effectively used for supplementary material for the classroom teacher, some of the longer songs are suitable for special school programs. As an added feature, a child chosen for his/her speaking ability will enjoy reading alone or reciting by memory the interesting facts about each composer before the group sings the song.

Suggested grade levels are listed on page 7.

It is my hope that this book may help children grow in their musical experience and may help them to know and to love music of the great composers.

Mary Margaret Clark

ALPHABETICAL INDEX OF COMPOSERS

SUGGESTED GRADE LEVEL

FOR FALL

ON HALLOWEEN
(FROM DANSE MACABRE)
By Camille Saint-Saëns

Saint-Saëns was a French composer, born in Paris in 1835. He lived until 1921. Saint-Saëns had many interests besides music. He was also an astronomer, poet, mathematician, and archaeologist. Many people like his music because he wrote with a sense of humor.

(For more information on his life, see page *65*.)

Moderato
1. When- e'er I see a ghost go by, I
2. I think to- night on Hal- low- een, you'll
mp
hear------his sad--------and mourn- ful cry. I'd
see an old witch who is ver- y mean. A-
like to be a ghost so bold, and
cross the dark and som- ber sky, you'll
cres.

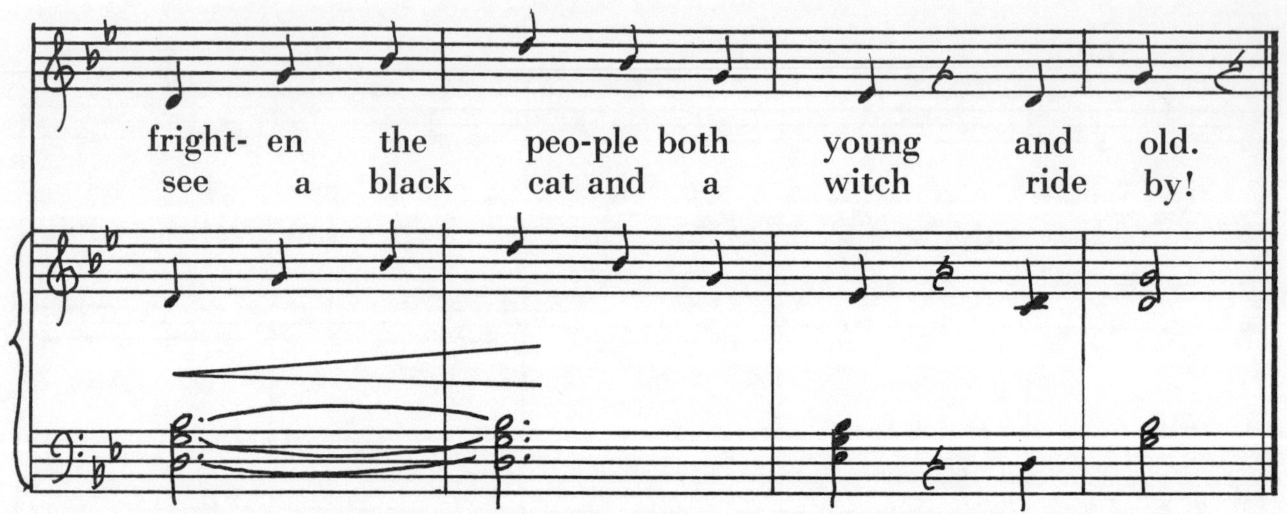
fright- en the peo-ple both young and old.
see a black cat and a witch ride by!

'TIS THE NIGHT OF HALLOWEEN
(FROM FUNERAL MARCH, SONATA, B♭ MINOR)

By Frederic Chopin

Frederic Chopin was born near Warsaw, Poland, in 1810. He was a wonderful pianist and has often been called "the Poet of the Piano." He was a marvelously gifted child and began his concert appearances at the age of nine. He was a very patriotic person and greatly loved his native Poland. He was a young man when he died—only thirty-nine. He had contracted tuberculosis and was too weak to overcome it.

Ghosts in their shrouds start to shim- mer in- to sight.
Oo- oo- oo- oo- oo- oo- oo- oo- oo- oo- oo.
Witches on their broom-sticks, fly- in' through the air----
Spooks be- gin to howl------- Cats are on the prowl---
cres.
f
Bats flap their wings as they scat- ter ev'- ry- where.
Eyes mean and green. 'Tis the night of Hal- lo- ween. (Fine)
mp
Rit.

Moderato
mf Tall skel-e-tons are walk- ing by. Fall leaves are blowing
mf
from on high. See yel-low pump- kins
burn- ing big and bright, and hear the wind moan sad-ly in the dark night.
Ritard

ON THANKSGIVING DAY
(FROM THE "NEW WORLD SYMPHONY")

By Anton Dvořák

Anton Dvořák was born in Bohemia in 1841. As a boy he loved music and spent much of his time playing the violin and singing in the church choir. Although his father wanted his son to enjoy music, he did not want him to follow it as an occupation.

Because Anton was extremely talented and loved music so much, however, he eventually went to the city of Prague to study music.

Many people recognized his great ability. One very important person who wanted to help Dvořák was Johannes Brahms. Brahms used his position and fame to help further the career of Anton.

After becoming famous for his music writing, Dvořák came to the United States in 1885 to become the director of the National Conservatory of Music in New York. He loved America, but often he was homesick. In the summertime he visited Spillville, Iowa, where many other Bohemians lived. It was in Spillville that he wrote his famous "New World Symphony."

Many persons interpret this symphony to sound distinctly American. Part of it sounds Indian, and part of it reflects Negro folk music, they say.

Others point out that it is very Bohemian.

Whatever it is, it is a beautiful symphony which Americans love.

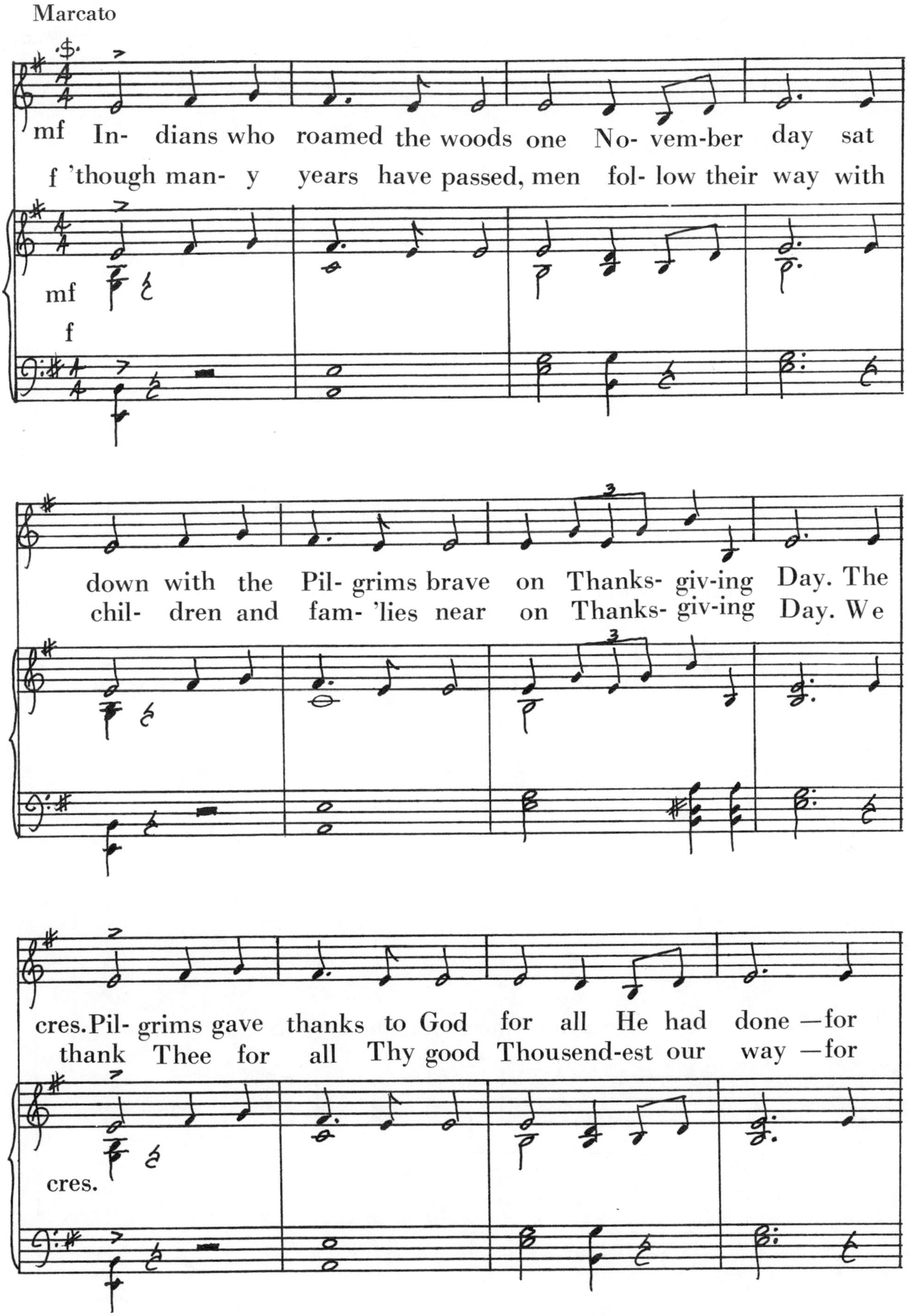

Marcato
mf In- dians who roamed the woods one No- vem-ber day sat
f 'though man- y years have passed, men fol- low their way with
mf
f
down with the Pil- grims brave on Thanks- giv-ing Day. The
chil- dren and fam- 'lies near on Thanks- giv-ing Day. We
3
cres. Pil- grims gave thanks to God for all He had done —for
thank Thee for all Thy good Thousend-est our way —for
cres.

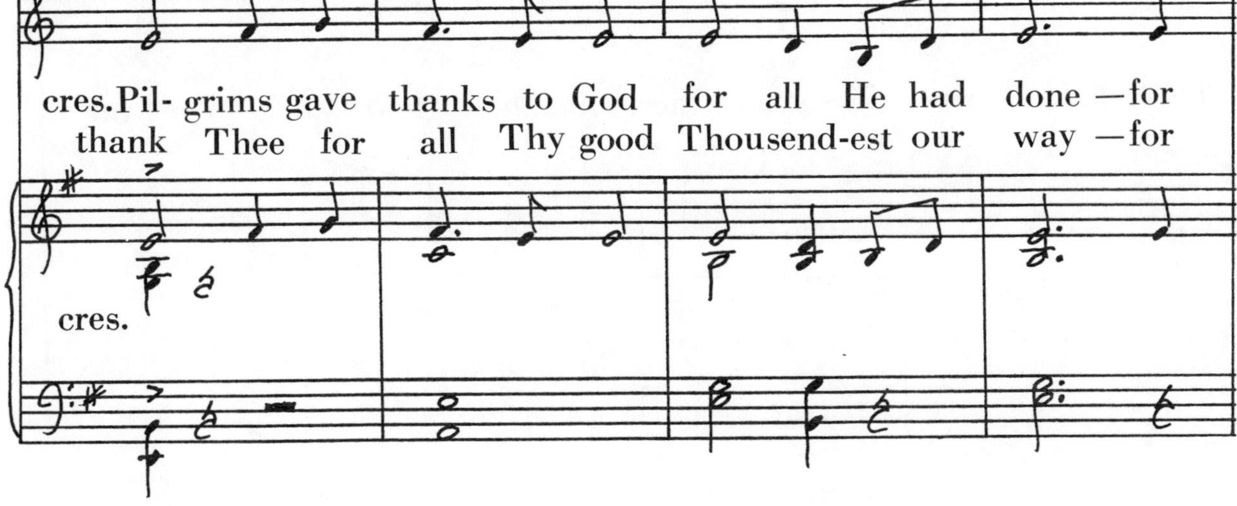

food and His good- ness great and for rain and sun.
love and for broth- er- hood on Thanks- giv- ing Day.
mp In- dians were thank-ful, too. Join- ing in hand, they
mp
thanked God with Pil- grims there for this great land. And

INDIAN DANCE

f
f
acc.
sfz

HEAR US NOW WE PRAY
(FROM PRELUDE IN C MINOR)
By Frederic Chopin

Largo
mf Teach us, Lord, to pray on Thanks- giv- ing Day.
mf
Grate-ful we may be for our coun- try free.
mp For Thy love and care, bow we now in prayer.
mp
cres.

For information on the life of Chopin, see page 14.

FOR WINTER

WINTER IS COMING
(FROM SYMPHONY NO. 5)

By Peter Tchaikovsky

Peter Tchaikovsky was born in Russia in 1840. He studied to be a lawyer; but at the age of twenty-two, he gave up law to be a musician. He used Russian folk tunes as a basis for many of his compositions. Tchaikovsky was a very sensitive and shy person. His music is very emotional, melodious, and beautiful. His music is especially popular in the United States.

Andante

flown the day- light hours--. Cold winds are
blow-ing. Soon 'twill be snow- ing. Gone are the
cres.
hours of light, the sun shin- ing bright. But 'til the
mf

spring comes-- un- til new life hums-- we will find
acc.
joy through win- ter hours. The fires will be
cres.
dim.
glow-ing, while it is snow-ing. Spring will ar-

Rit. rive one day with flow'rs.
Rit.

SNOWFLAKES
(FROM TRAUMEREI)

By Robert Schumann

Robert Schumann was born in Saxony in 1810 and composed his first musical composition at the age of seven.

He grew up and married a lovely and gifted concert pianist. Their married life was very happy and romantic, and his wife was the inspiration for many of the beautiful songs he wrote.

Schumann's life ended tragically, however, for before his death, he became mentally ill. He died when he was forty-six years old.

Andante

snow-flakes as they fall so peace-ful- ly.
fire-place watch-ing snowflakes peace-ful- ly.
Ritard

A CHRISTMAS SONG: GOD'S LOVE FROM ABOVE
(FROM "THE UNFINISHED SYMPHONY")

By Franz Schubert

Franz Schubert was born near Vienna, Austria, in 1797. Although he was a teacher by profession, he did not enjoy teaching, and he spent all of his spare time writing music. During his short life he wrote over six hundred songs.

He died when he was only thirty-two, but he left the world some of its most beautiful music. "Ave Maria" is one of his best loved songs.

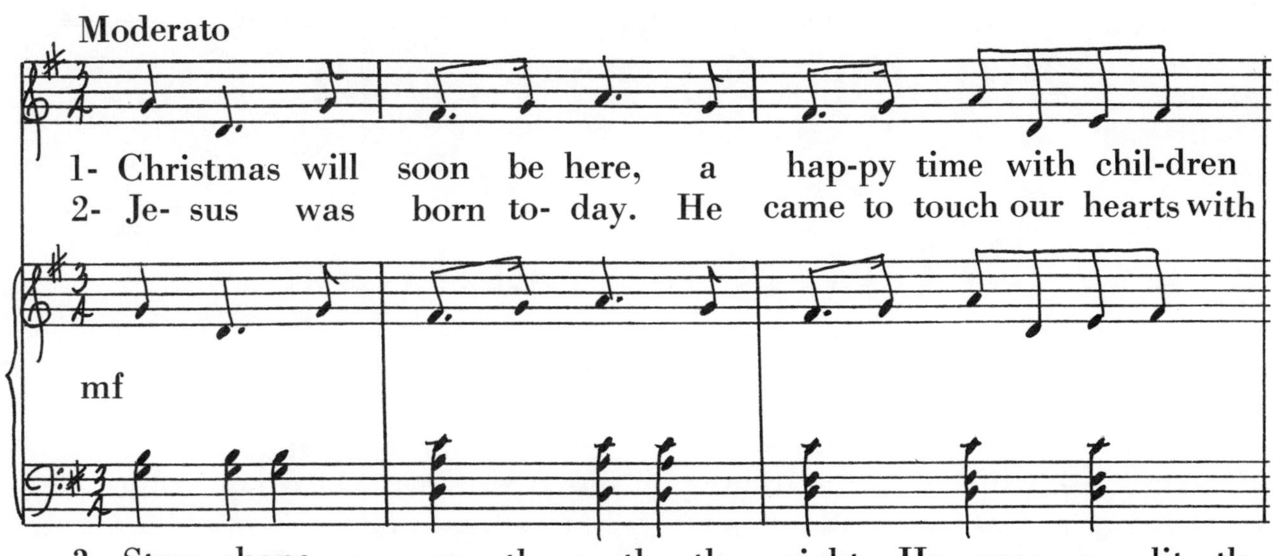
Moderato
1- Christmas will soon be here, a hap-py time with chil-dren
2- Je- sus was born to- day. He came to touch our hearts with
mf
3- Stars shone up- on the earth the night He was a lit- tle
(Play the third verse an octave higher.)

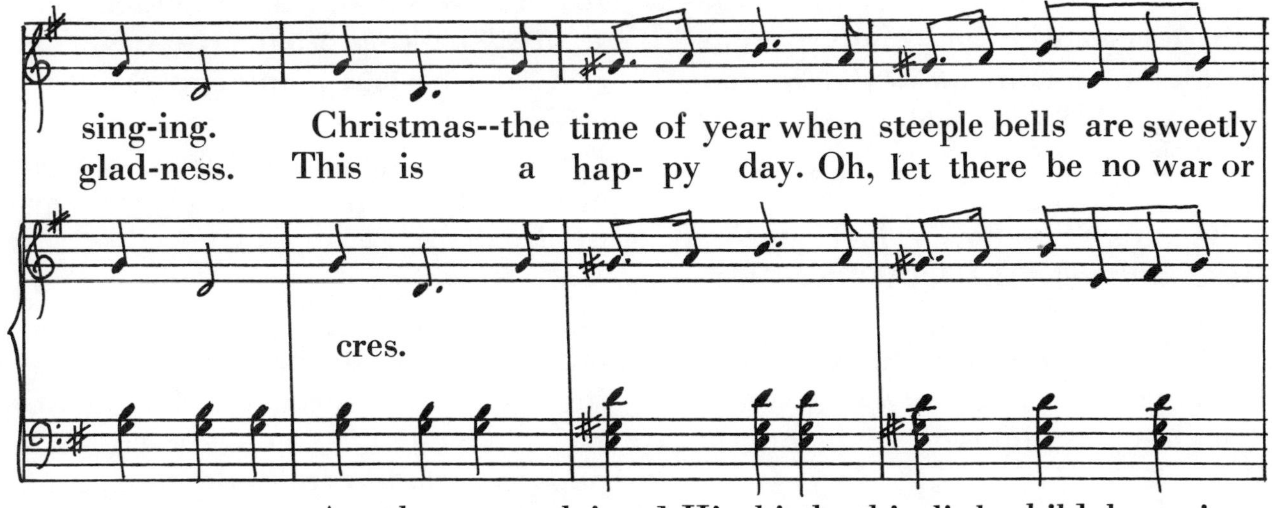
sing-ing. Christmas--the time of year when steeple bells are sweetly
glad-ness. This is a hap- py day. Oh, let there be no war or
cres.
stranger. Angels pro-claimed His birth--this little child born in a

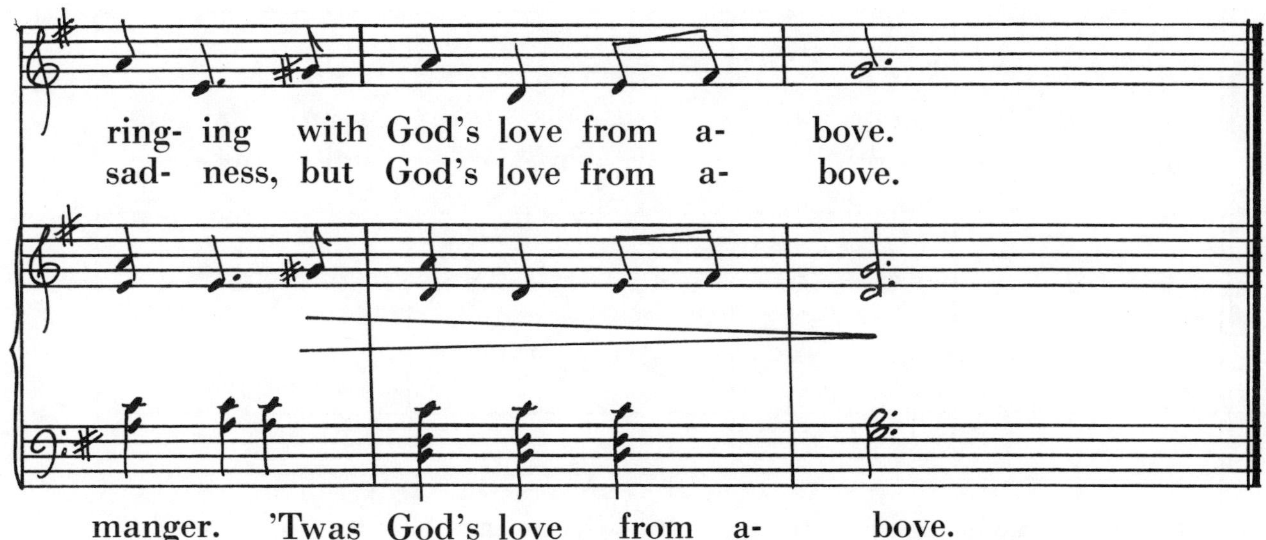
ring- ing with God's love from a- bove.
sad- ness, but God's love from a- bove.
manger. 'Twas God's love from a- bove.
(Ritard. third verse)

BE OF GOOD CHEER
(FROM THE SEVENTH SYMPHONY)

By Ludwig van Beethoven

Ludwig van Beethoven was born in Bonn, Germany, on December 16, 1770. If you were to go to Bonn today, you could visit his birthplace at 20 Bonngasse Street. Here are kept many relics of his lifetime, including his piano. The piano is roped off so that visitors cannot touch it. Thousands of people visit there each year and many persons would love to touch the keyboard that once belonged to the great Beethoven.

Like Brahms, Beethoven had an unhappy childhood. His father was very cruel and made him practice the piano much of the day and into the wee hours of the night. He used his young son to earn money for himself and for the family.

Beethoven had no childhood friends and no time ever to play. His best friend was his mother, and he was brokenhearted when she died while he was yet very young.

As a man, Beethoven was lonely and shy. He was not what might be called a good-looking man. He never married, and he had many sorrows.

He showed signs of deafness at the early age of thirty-one. Later he became totally deaf.

You may ask, How can a deaf man write music? But write he did. His wonderful talent far surpassed his deafness. He is loved and remembered as perhaps the greatest composer of all times.

1. this is a time to be of good cheer.
1. scenes of the Yule- tide this time of year.
cres.
2. Sleigh bells are ring- ing this time of year.
2. San- ta is bend- ing, lend- ing an ear.
1. Snow fall- ing light- ly-- trees spar- kling bright-ly.
1. Church bells are ring- ing. Chil- dren are sing- ing,
cres.
cres.
2. So let each broth- er love one an- oth- er.
2. Church bells are ring- ing. Chil- dren are sing- ing,
1.
1. Songs of the Sea- son--- car- ol- ing clear.
1. "Be of good cheer for
P
2. Let there be peace on earth far and near.
2. "Be of good cheer for Christ- mas is here."

2.
Christ- mas is here."
Ritard.

SOLDIERS IN THE SNOW
(FROM MARCH SLAV)

By Peter Tchaikovsky

f
sol-diers march on in the snow.
f
Dark gray is the sky, as the day-light flies swiftly
mf
by. While the i- cy win-ter winds are blowing,
cres.
cres.

march they ev-er, stop-ping never, through the snow.

For the life of Tchaikovsky, see page 29.

FOR SPRING

SPRING SONG
By Felix Mendelssohn

Felix Mendelssohn was born in Hamburg, Germany, in 1809. He must have worked very hard as a child; for in later years, he recalled how much he enjoyed Sundays because on that day he was not made to get up at five o'clock to practice.

He wrote many great religious works. Among them are the oratorios, "Elijah" and "St. Paul." He was always a blithe and happy person, yet very modest. Nearly all great men of his day knew and loved Mendelssohn.

Moderato
mf
1. Hear the lit-tle bird that sings his mel- o-
2. Hear the love- ly pit- ter pat- ter of the
mf
dy. He knows that win- ter time is o'er and
rain. It falls up- on the flow- er seeds and
spring is gently com- ing. I hear the lit-tle
soon they will be grow- ing. I see a love-ly
Rit.
A Tempo

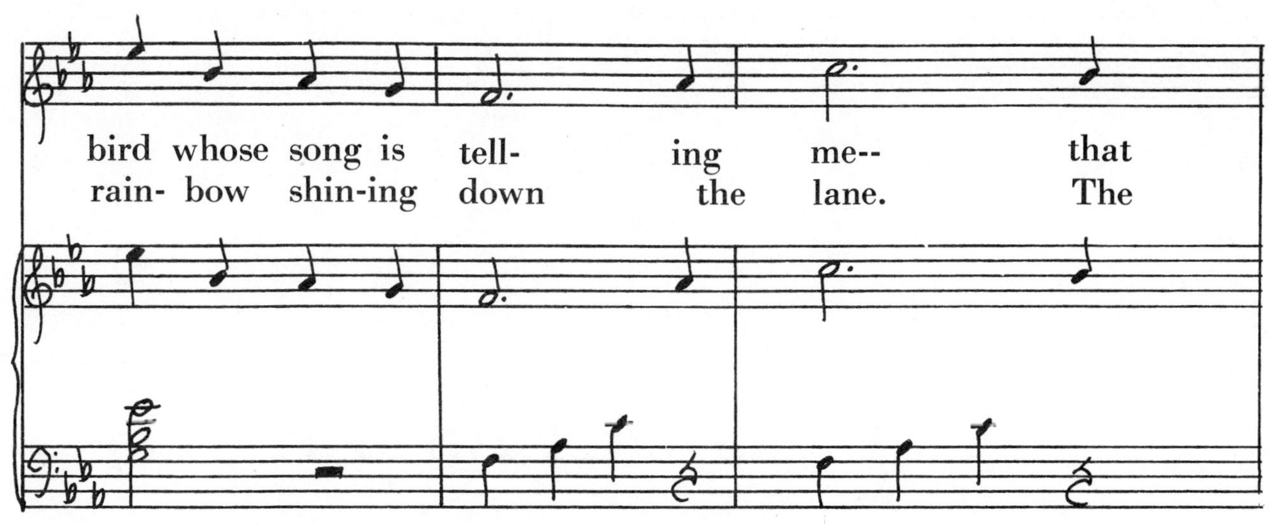
bird whose song is tell- ing me-- that
rain- bow shin-ing down the lane. The

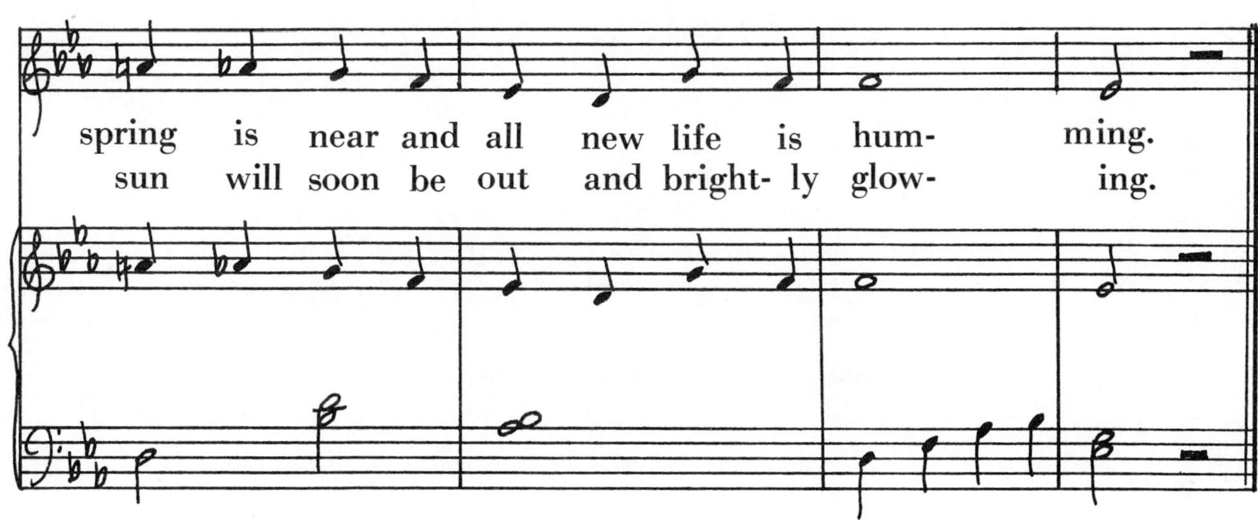
spring is near and all new life is hum- ming.
sun will soon be out and bright- ly glow- ing.

BELLS OF EASTER
(FROM PRELUDE IN A MAJOR)

By Frederic Chopin

Frederic Chopin was born near Warsaw, Poland, in 1810. He wrote many beautiful compositions for the piano, and was called the "Poet of the Piano." He was a brilliant child and began his concert appearances at the age of nine.

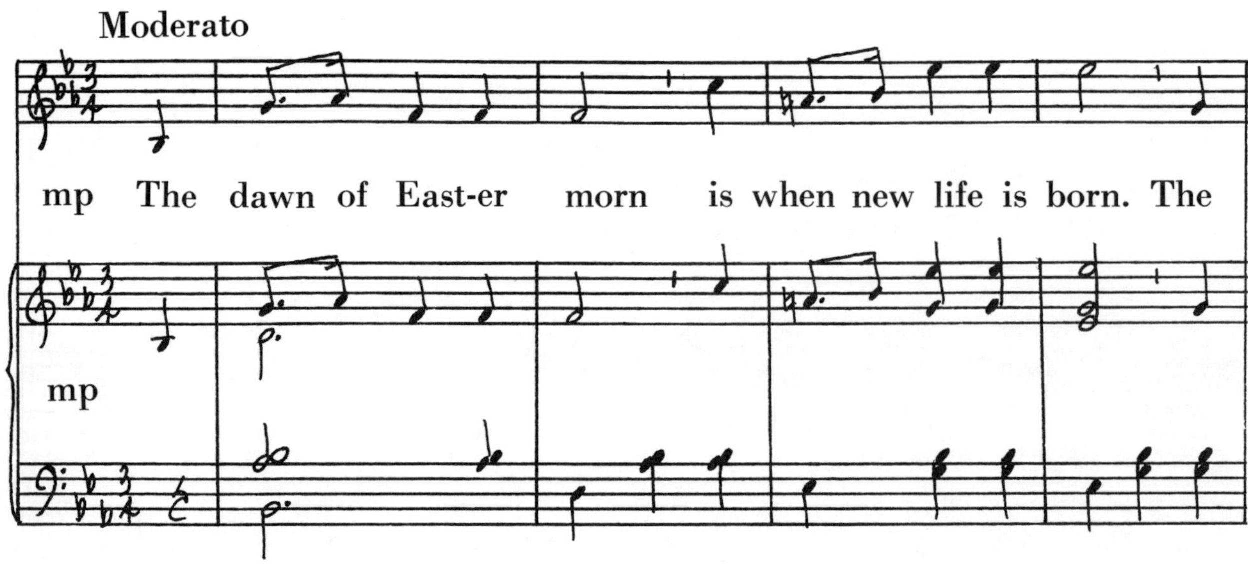

bud-ding flow'rs and grass bring word that win-ter's past.
cres.
(Sing)
(Children ring triangles or bells in time to music) So,
cres.
Ritard
bells of East-er, ring; and ush- er in the spring!
Ritard
Ritard

FOR SUMMER

SWINGING WHILE IT RAINS
(FROM DIE FLEDERMAUS)

By Johann Strauss

Although Johann Strauss, Jr., was the son of a musician, his father objected bitterly to his son's studying music. Therefore, Johann Strauss, Jr., studied music in secret for many years. He became a successful musician in spite of his father and later became known as the "Waltz King."

Among his many compositions are "The Blue Danube Waltz," "Tales from the Vienna Woods," and "The Fledermaus."

Strauss was born in 1825 in Vienna, Austria, and died there in 1899. During his lifetime he toured with his orchestra, going to many famous cities in Europe and America.

Happily
1. Hear the splish and splat-ter, hear the pit- ter pat- ter
2. Hear the splish and splat-ter, hear the pit- ter pat- ter
mf
(On the repeat, play the first eight measures "piano" an octave higher.)
of the sum- mer rain. Hur- ry up and pull the
of the sum- mer rain. Tra- la- la- la- la- la
win- dows down, bang! Hur- ry up and pull the windows down, bang!
(clap clap clap clap) Tra- la- la- la- la- la- (clap clap clap clap)

1-2 Riv- u- lets are run- ning, riv- u lets are run-ning
down the win- dow- pane. Tra- la- la- la- la- la
la- la- la- la. Lis- ten to the sum- mer rain!

f Now, we will sit on the porch and swing.
f
Girls
Watch- ing the rain, we will gay- ly sing!
Boys
'Though out- of- doors we can- not go play,

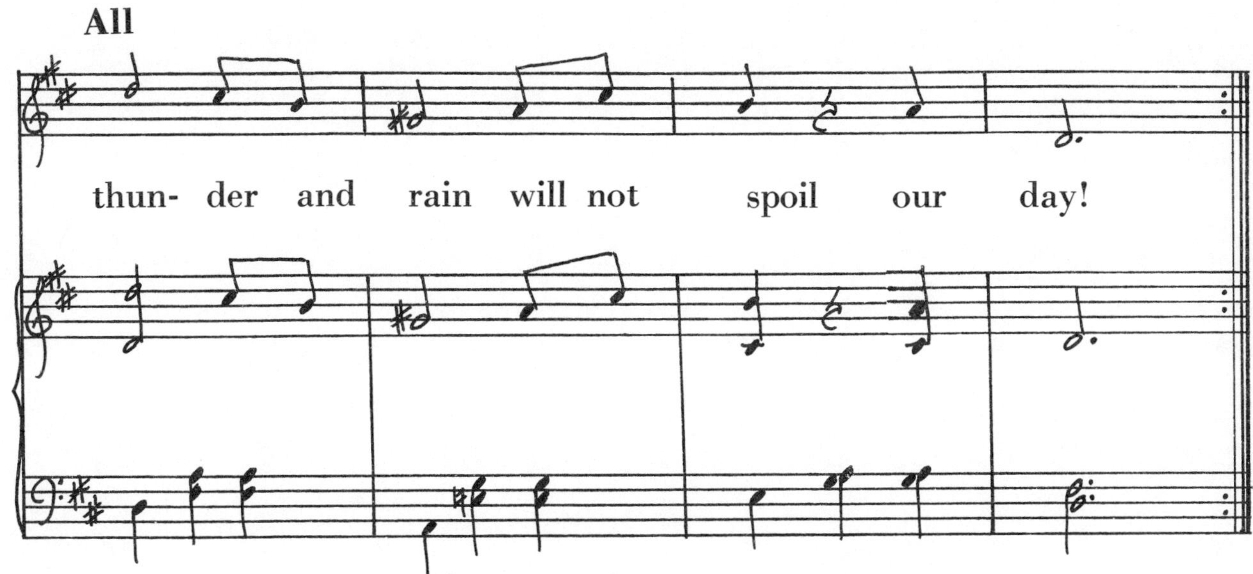

(Not so many years ago, many houses in our country were built with large front porches. In the South especially, many of these porches held a large, family size swing. On rainy days, the front porch with its large swing was a delightful place for children to play. Many happy hours were there spent—swinging, singing, giggling, and playing games.)

OTHER SONGS FROM

MUSIC OF GREAT COMPOSERS

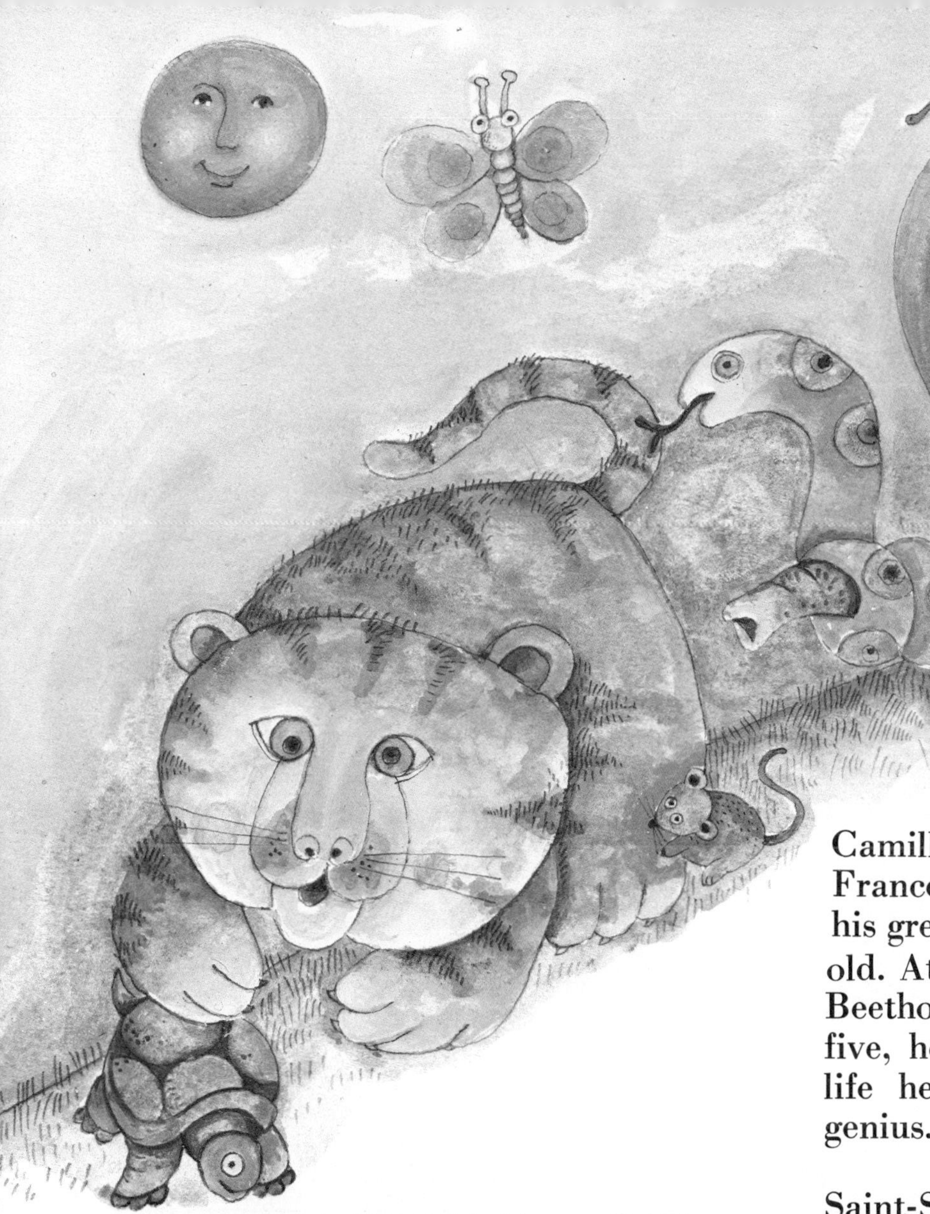

CARNIVAL OF ANIMALS

(FROM FINALE OF CARNIVAL OF ANIMALS)

Camille Saint-Saëns

When Camille Saint-Saëns was still an infant, his mother realized that he was very sensitive to musical sounds. When he heard a pleasant tone, Camille's face would light up. When he heard a discord, the baby would frown with an expression of pain.

Camille Saint-Saëns was born in Paris, France, in 1835. He studied piano from his great-aunt before he was three years old. At four-and-a-half, he could play a Beethoven sonata. By the time he was five, he was composing music. All his life he was recognized as a musical genius.

Saint-Saëns had many interests besides music. He wrote books on literature and painting. He studied astronomy and natural history. He produced a play and wrote poetry. For the most part, his life was an unusually happy and successful one.

Tragedy came to him, however, when his little boy fell from a window and was killed. His second child died a few weeks later.

After this great sorrow, Saint-Saëns traveled extensively. He gave many concerts directing his own music, traveling all over the world. He came to the United States in 1906 and again in 1916.

mf Mule and kan- ga- roo with a lion and a bird and cuckoo,
mf
too, with the el- e- phants are com- ing two by
two in the Car-ni- val of An- i- mals a-long with hens and

cocks and fos- sils march-ing down the av- e- nue and
street. See them com-ing with a loud and nois- y
beat. They are strum-ming to the pian- o play- er's

beat in the Car- ni- val of An- i- mals. C'est c'est si bon, si
(Say) (Bohn)
bon, si bon, the mu- sic of Ca- mille Saint-Saëns!
(Bohn) (Săn-Sähn)

MUSIC BY TCHAIKOVSKY
(FROM SLEEPING BEAUTY WALTZ)

By Peter Tchaikovsky

Peter Tchaikovsky was born in Russia in 1840. He became one of the world's greatest composers of music. Tchaikovsky's music has been popular especially in the United States. "Sleeping Beauty Waltz" is from the ballet, "Sleeping Beauty."

He was a man with very deep and sensitive feelings, and these emotions are reflected in the beautiful melodies he wrote. Though successful in his musical career, he lived a lonely life; and at times, this loneliness, too, is reflected in his music.

Peter Tchaikovsky wrote six symphonies.

He came to the United States in 1891 and conducted his own "1812 Overture" at the opening of Carnegie Hall.

He died in 1893.

"Sleep- ing Beau- ty Waltz."
Love- ly mel- o- dy has been
cres.
writ- ten by a man named Tchai- kov- sky. And
Ritard

he could write the love- li-est
A Tempo
mel- o- dies of all! Sleeping
Beau- ty--- she is danc- ing! She is
f
f

danc- ing at the ball!

MUSIC BY CHOPIN
(FROM "MINUTE WALTZ," OP. 64, NO. 1)

By Frederic Chopin

Frederic Chopin was one of the greatest pianists who ever lived. Not only did he write music for the piano, but he could also play the piano magnificently well. He gave concert tours in every important city in Europe. As a child, he was brilliant and gave concerts at a very early age. He was still a young man when he died of tuberculosis.

Moderato
1. Lis- ten to the "Min- ute Waltz,"
2. Po- land was his na- tive land--
mp
writ- ten by a man whose name was Cho-pin.
proud to claim this man named Fred' ric Cho-pin.
cres.
Rit.
He could write when he was young---
Born in eight- teen hund- dred ten---
A tempo
cres.

f
mu- sic great, the whole world has sung.
"Pian- o Po- et," great a- mong men!
f

HOPE, COURAGE, AND HONOR
(FROM POMP AND CIRCUMSTANCE)

By Edward Elgar

Edward Elgar was a great English composer of music. He was born near Worcester, England, in 1857, and died in 1934.

His wife was a woman of remarkable vision, and she encouraged Edward Elgar to be the great musician and composer he was.

"Pomp and Circumstance, March No. 2 in A Minor" is almost as intimately associated with the British Empire as "God Save the King." All British people love this beautiful march.

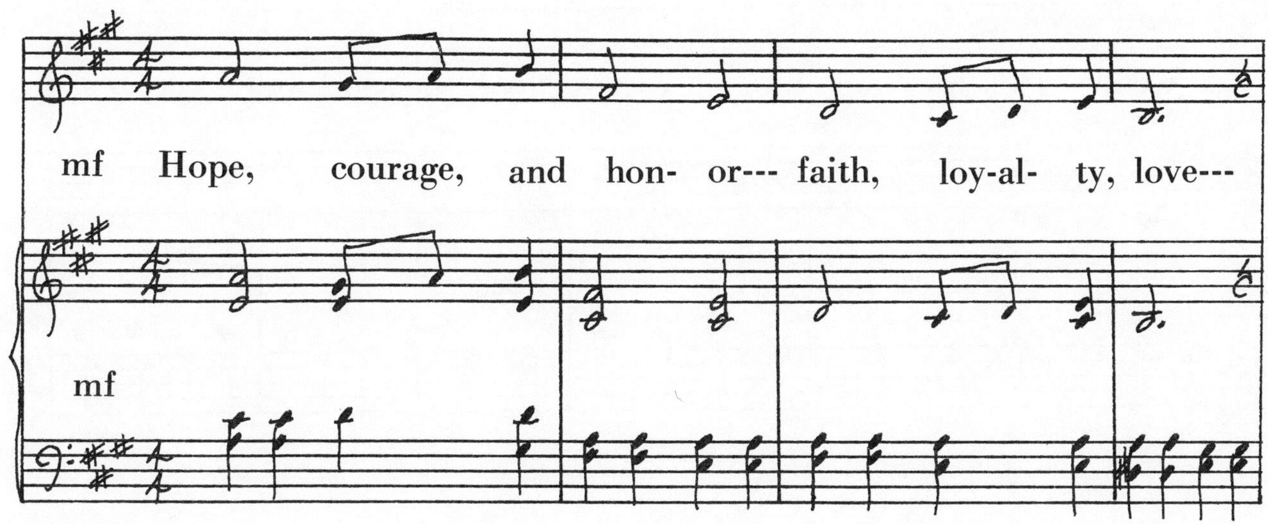

These things have been giv- en from God up a- bove.
f *Come sad-ness and sor- row, grief, worry, or woe,
f
*we'll look for to- mor- row--- *look forward and know---
cres.

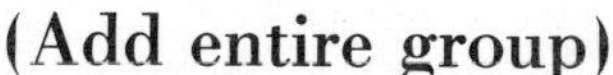

....

The above song makes a good program number.

* At the beginning, have all singers participate moderately loud. Next, repeat the music, beginning softly with only two or three outstanding singers. At each asterisk add several children until the entire group is singing loudly together at the end. This creates a special "build-up" effect.

GYPSIES DANCING
(FROM "HUNGARIAN DANCE NO. 6")

By Johannes Brahms

Johannes Brahms was born in Hamburg, Germany, in 1833. Although he experienced an unhappy childhood, Brahms grew up to become one of the greatest composers who ever lived.

His family lived in poverty in a crowded tenement on the waterfront of Hamburg; and as a child, Johannes often went hungry. His mother, who was slightly deformed, took in sewing to help earn money for the family. His parents often fought bitterly. There was no happy home atmosphere for him as a little boy.

Yet, in spite of these unhappy circumstances, Johannes Brahms rose above his misfortune to become one of the greatest loved composers the world has ever known.

Moderately Fast

shout, "Hi Ho." --- a- clap-ping in a hur- ry!
"Hi! Hi! Ho!" Not a wor- ry ---- they
know as they go, dancing so!

PATRIOTS WILL ANSWER
(FROM POLONAISE NO. 3 IN A MAJOR)

By Frederic Chopin

Sing lively; but do not attempt to sing as fast as the piano solo. Children in the fourth grades and higher will enjoy the challenge of learning the words and music to this stirring polonaise.

Pa- tri- ots will answer when their duty calls! (Drum)
3
Men an-swer the sound of trum-pets call- ing
forth to arm. From the cit- y and the

Fine
farm, spir-its a- rise when dan-ger lies where our flag flies!
Boys
mp
If ----------but war should cease, men could
But -----------'til war shall cease, men can't
mp
All
live in peace---------- lov- ing their coun-try, serv-ing,
live in peace. Through storm- y weath-er brave men
cres.

For information on the life of Chopin see pages 14, 24, 52, and 74.

SNOW WHITE SMILES
(FROM A MINOR PIANO CONCERTO)

By Edvard Grieg

Edvard Grieg was born in Bergen, Norway, in 1843. As a little boy, he did not do well in school. Some of his teachers even considered him to be lazy and stupid. He was often in trouble and was frequently sent home from school.

Edvard did not like practicing the piano, either. It was too much work, he thought. Yet, this indolent boy grew up to become Norway's greatest and best loved musician and composer.

Grieg was able to accomplish this not only because he had great talent, but also because as he grew up, he changed his ways and became an extremely hard worker in everything he undertook.

Edvard Grieg became a national hero in his native land because the "soul of Norway" sang in his music. Many of his famous compositions include folk-like melodies of Norway.

All the people loved him. When he died, in 1907, more than four hundred thousand Norwegians lined the streets in Bergen to pay homage to him. Today he is loved not only in Norway but throughout the world.

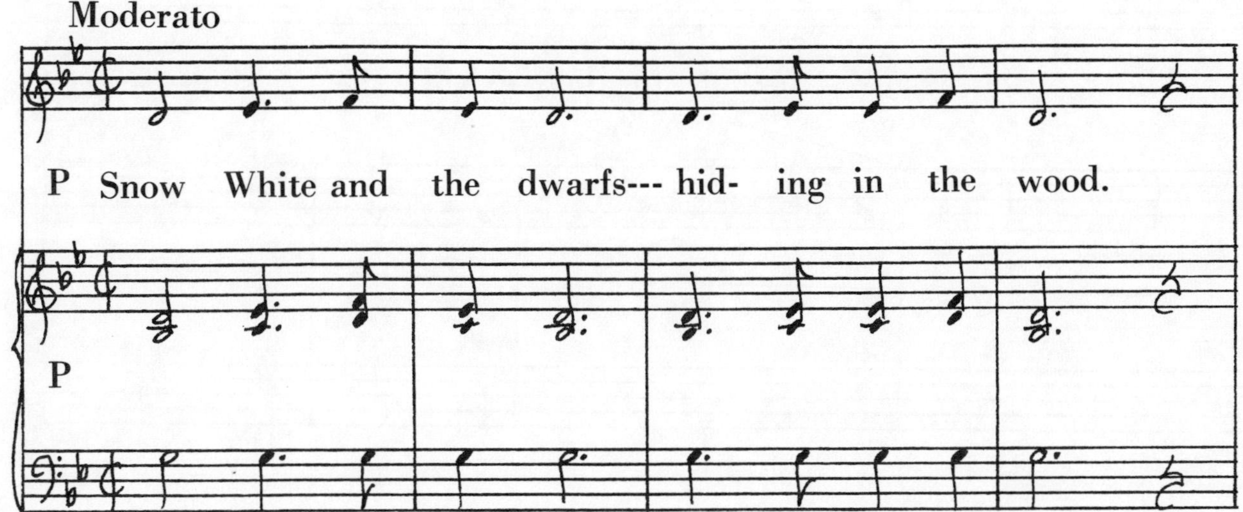

mf Snow White and the dwarfs---hid- ing in the wood.
mf
Snow White smiles; joy she brings.
3
All the birds lis-ten to her when she sings---.
3

When I smile, joy it brings.
Like Snow White I shall think on ver-y pleas- ant things.
3
3
Rit.

EDVARD GRIEG
(FROM A MINOR PIANO CONCERTO)

By Edvard Grieg

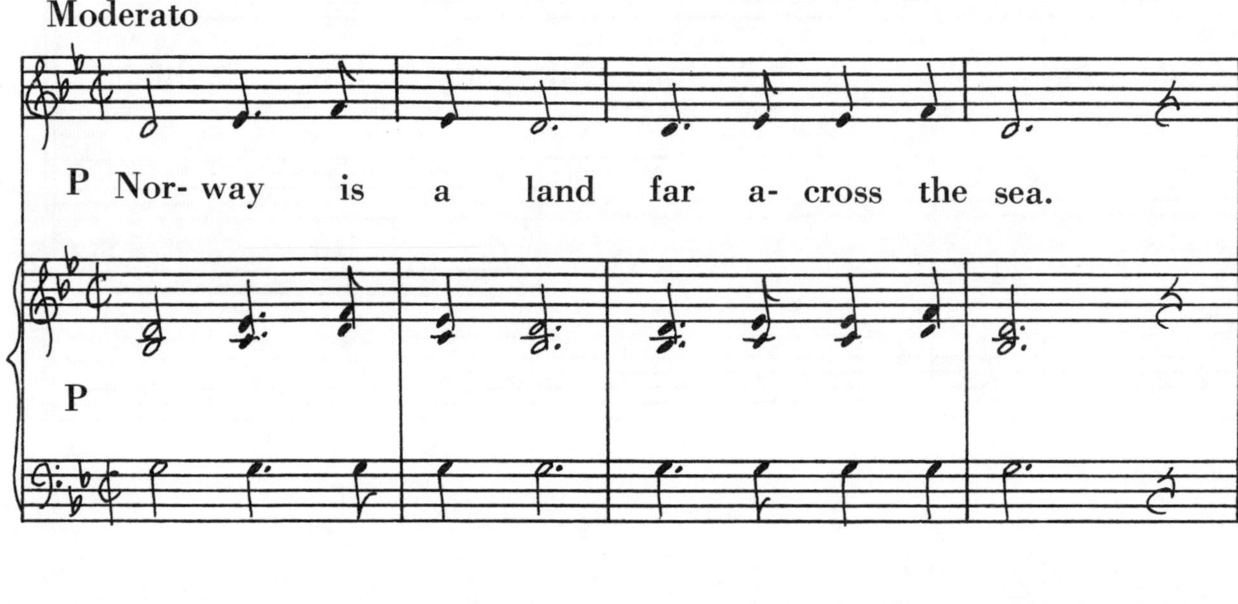

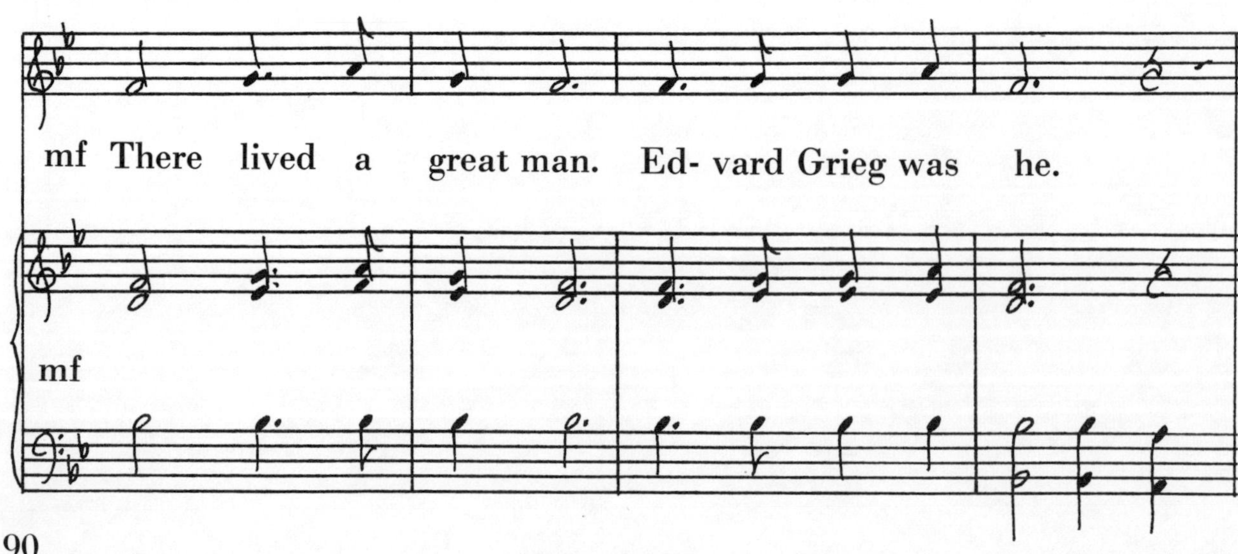

Born to write mu- sic bright.
3
All the peo-ple in Nor- way loved his bring-ing
3
mu- sic grand to their land.

3
How his coun-try and all the world loved Ed- vard Grieg!
3

THE PARADE
(FROM SOLDIERS' CHORUS FROM THE OPERA "FAUST")
By Charles Gounod

Charles Gounod was a little boy when he decided that he wanted to devote his life to studying music. One of his adult friends asked him why he wished to do this.

"Because I love music," was his reply.

So at the age of five, Charles began his study of the subject he loved most.

As Gounod grew up, he became a very religious person, and because of this, he wrote much religious music. One of his most beautiful pieces is "Ave Maria," based on "Prelude in C Major" by Bach.

He is remembered also for his wonderful operas. His best loved one is "Faust," which broght him world-wide fame.

Charles Gounod was born in Paris, France, in 1818. At seventy-five, he died in 1893, a man who had spent his life in the profession he chose at the age of five.

March Tempo

f
1-Sol-diers are marching a- long the street--sol- diers in
2-We'll see the sol----diers on pa-rade. We'll hear the
f
time to the drum-mer's beat. Now hear the
mu-sic and rhyme that's made. Now hear the
tum---ing of the drum, "Ta- rat- a- ta-tat, a-rat----a- ta-
tum---ing of the drum, "Ta- rat- a- ta-tat, a-rat----a- ta-

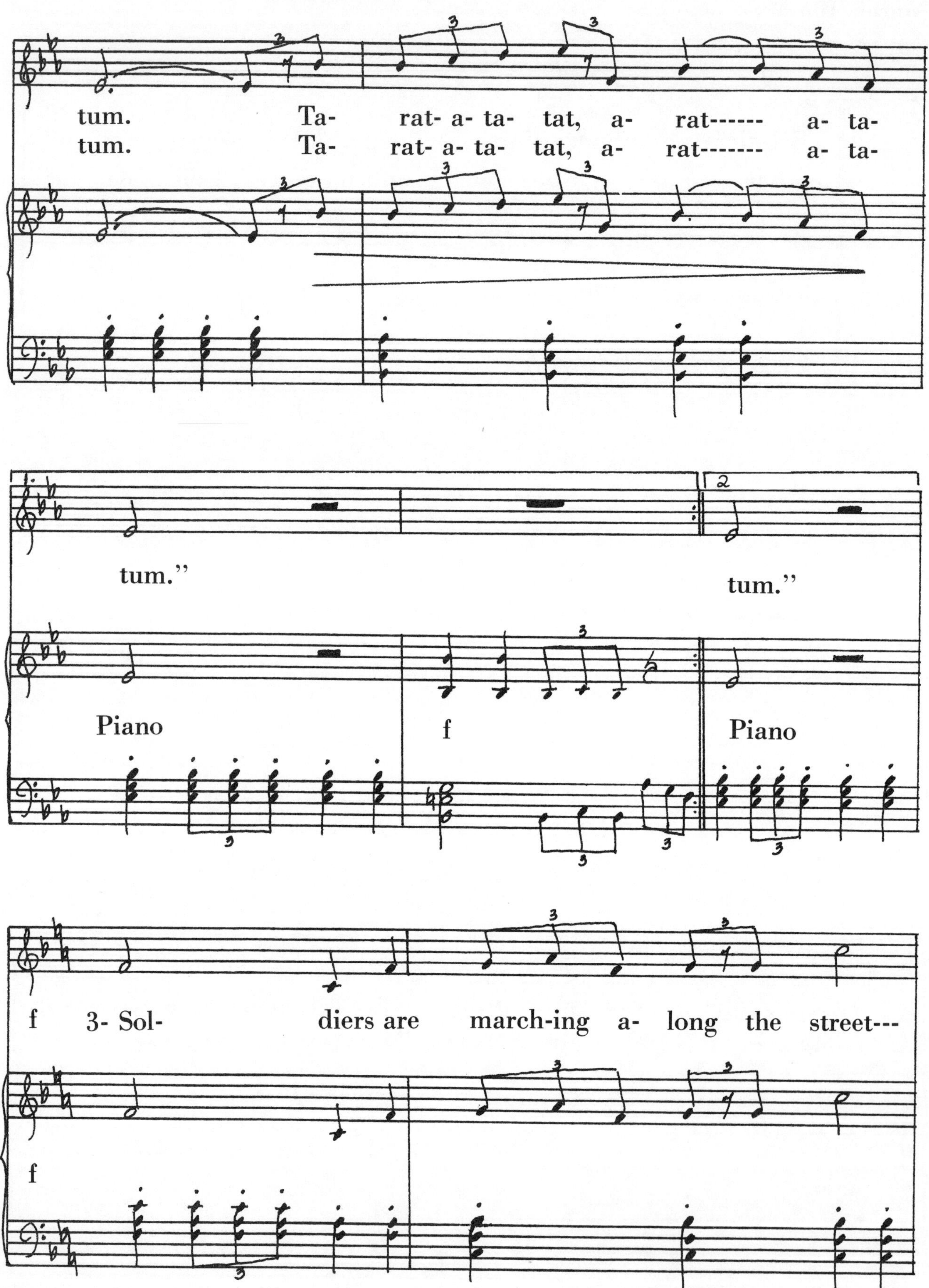
tum. Ta- rat- a- ta- tat, a- rat------ a- ta-
tum. Ta- rat- a- ta- tat, a- rat------ a- ta-
tum.''
tum.''
Piano
f
Piano
f 3- Sol- diers are march-ing a- long the street---
f

sol- diers in time to the drum- mer's beat. Now hear the
tum------ing of the drum, "Ta- rat- a- ta- tat, a- rat-- a-ta-
tum. Ta- rat- a- ta- tat, a- rat----a-ta- tum!"
Piano